Soap Making: Reviving a Lost Art!

How to Make Homemade Soap like a Pro

By: Mindy Jackson

PUBLISHERS NOTES

Disclaimer

This publication is intended to provide helpful and informative material. It is not intended to diagnose, treat, cure, or prevent any health problem or condition, nor is it intended to replace the advice of a physician. No action should be taken solely on the contents of this book. Always consult your physician or qualified health-care professional on any matters regarding your health and before adopting any suggestions in this book or drawing inferences from it.

The author and publisher specifically disclaim all responsibility for any liability, loss or risk, personal or otherwise, which is incurred as a consequence, directly or indirectly, from the use or application of any contents of this book.

Any and all product names referenced within this book are the trademarks of their respective owners. None of these owners have sponsored, authorized, endorsed, or approved this book.

Always read all information provided by the manufacturers' product labels before using their products. The author and publisher are not responsible for claims made by manufacturers.

Paperback Edition

Manufactured in the United States of America

Dedication

This text is dedicated to my mother June and my Aunt Sarah. They got me into the habit of doing things myself and it has made me quite an independent young woman.

TABLE OF CONTENTS

PUBLISHERS NOTES 2

DEDICATION 3

TABLE OF CONTENTS 4

CHAPTER 1- HOMEMADE SOAP-A BRIEF HISTORY 5

CHAPTER 2- THE BENEFITS OF HOMEMADE SOAP 12

CHAPTER 3- FOUR METHODS OF MAKING HOMEMADE SOAP 20

CHAPTER 4- THE EQUIPMENT NEEDED TO MAKE HOMEMADE SOAP 29

CHAPTER 5- SAFETY MEASURES TO TAKE WHEN MAKING HOMEMADE SOAP 36

CHAPTER 6- ADDING COLORS AND SCENTS TO HOMEMADE SOAP 43

CHAPTER 7- GREAT HOMEMADE SOAP RECIPES 49

ABOUT THE AUTHOR 57

Chapter 1 - Homemade Soap - A Brief History

The making of soap would have been a task that was very familiar to many early Americans, as imported products form Europe were either not affordable or not available to the average person living in this country before the industrial revolution. Today, a whole new class of artisans, environmentally concerned citizens, as well as those desiring a simpler way of life, are all bringing this once common tradition back into the fold of everyday life. This chapter will focus on the small scale productions for home use exemplified by the small batch production that is utilized for homemade production. The earliest records of soap making on any scale, date back to ancient Babylon. A recipe for soap making has even survived from that time. The ingredients of that ancient soap included water, oil, and alkali, items that are intimately familiar to anyone in the modern age choosing to make their own product.

What truly separates modern homemade soap making from mass production is the extensive use of the cold process or the semi-boiled process for production in the former and the use of the fully hot process in the later. It should be noted that in most cases, homemade producers utilize the cold process over the semi boiled one. In either case an excess of oil or fat is always utilized to ensure the full reaction of alkali, almost always sodium hydroxide (lye) or potassium hydroxide. The choice of alkali is based on the desired hardness of the finished product. Softer soaps as well as liquid ones require potassium hydroxide, while harder ones require sodium hydroxide. It is incredibly important that soap makers follow saponification charts to ensure that they are utilizing enough fat to react with the alkali salts to ensure their full usage as any leftovers in the final products will burn or irritate the skin of the user. Molds used in the final stages of production come in every shape and size imaginable and allow for soap makers to infuse creativity in their production.

The basis of all modern recipes for soap originated in the middle Ages where soap making technology was improved as production became the function of highly skilled guild workers. One of the innovators of modern homemade soap making, Ann Bramson constantly described the differences between store bought and the ones made following her recipes. She always spoke of the character that homemade soap has compared to the ones sold at drug stores. This perception of quality and character dominates the movement of homemade soap making that has its beginnings in the writing and activism of Bramson and others in the 1970s.

The 1970s saw the rise in popularity in the United States of the back-to-the-land movement that began as a rejection of the ever increasing urban character of modern life many decades earlier. The popularity of homemade soap making has continued to increase in the United States even as the back to the land movement has lost much of its steam. The attraction of making soap at home has captured the attention of many different kinds of people and there is no one ideology or political choice that drives the increasing numbers of individuals choosing to make their own soaps and detergents at home.

Today's homemade soap makers make many different varieties of soaps with Castile ones (made primarily of olive oil), ones made with goat milk, and several others being predominant. Users and the makers of these high quality, individually milled soaps speak to the same outstanding attributes that were so often staples of the writings of Ann Bramson and other advocates of homemade soap making including Ann Watson and Susan Miller. Homemade soap makers also report high rates of satisfaction from the work that goes into the production itself as well.

The popularity of homemade soap making can be easily attested to by way of a simple Google search for recipes of how to do so. Many of these include exotic ingredients including herbs, essential oils, and even rare vegetable oils such as tea, argon, and / or rosehip. Others abide by the motto simpler is better and include the previously mentioned Castile and goat milk soaps. Coconut oil is also starting to become a very popular ingredient due to the expansive coverage of the anti-inflammatory benefits of the oil. Other popular oils include those made from palm and butters made from Shea and cocoa. There exist many recipes that even preclude alkalis and are made from pure vegetable glycerin. These soaps are highly valued by many as they are vegan and extremely moisturizing. In addition, many makers prefer these glycerin recipes because they do not use any alkalis increasing the safety of the process.

One sure thing is that homemade soap making is becoming more popular and the number and variety of recipes for soaps being utilized is increasing every year. Whatever the recipe being used, homemade soaps continue to fascinate and provide their makers with great joy and satisfaction both of which will surely grow as the popularity of doing so grows and new exciting recipes are constantly being developed. Users of these soaps are the real lucky ones, as their cleaning and moisturizing qualities cannot be equalled by the unappealing bars available at the local drug store or grocery store.

Chapter 2 - The Benefits Of Homemade Soap

In this day and age many consumers have become aware of the added chemicals, increased costs, and commercial processes used to manufacture personal hygiene items, including the soap we use to bathe ourselves, and families, with daily. The big producers are adding things that are considered toxic, can encourage diseases, cancers and other previously less common problems, including added fragrances and dyes that can cause allergies and skin afflictions. Because of increased knowledge of these unnecessary additives, there is a popular movement, particularly among the growing population of Homesteaders, to make soap at home. There are many ways of doing this, and as mentioned in Chapter 1, a simple internet search will provide hundreds of recipes and methods. The majority of the recipes include the use of a combination of oils, and the addition of an agent to aid in the chemistry of soap making, such as lye. The recipes also generally include fragrances in the form of essential oils, and various other natural additives such as rosemary, oatmeal, lavender or corn meal. Making your own soap at home is one of the easiest steps you can take toward frugal living and creating a more natural and healthy environment for your family. In this chapter we will discuss the benefits of making your own soap in three ways. First, we will talk about the undesirable ingredients that are found in commercially produced soap. Second, we will discuss the preferable ingredients that you can use to make your own soap at home. And third, we will look into the frugality and personal satisfaction of being able to create your own products at home.

The Undesirable Ingredients

One of the most common reasons for making your own soap at home is the health benefits that come from homemade soap. Store bought products often contain things like Alkali, which is the most common irritant found in store bought soap. This petroleum based detergent will not only dry out your skin, it will also give you that tight feeling that comes from stripping your skin of its natural oils. This is what we, as consumers in a commercial world, have come to regard as "clean". Other undesirable chemical additives in this commercial soap include DEA, Alcohol, Triclosan, BHT and Isopropyl. None of these are recognized, or properly utilized, by the human body and should not be included in our daily regimen. Triclosan is one of the most concerning of these chemicals. It is usually found in anti-bacterial soap and is a culprit in preventing the body from creating its own strong immune system to fight off bacteria and infections. Although it has been used in products for over 30 years, recent studies are showing that the overuse of Triclosan has been proven to alter hormone regulation.

Commercially produced soap usually contain sodium tallowate, which is, simply put, tallow, or beef fat. Given this list of undesirable, and sometimes unknown, ingredients used to make commercial soap, it is only natural that we would want to explore more desirable, natural ingredients to use for making our own soap for ourselves and our families.

The Desirable Ingredients

Making your own soap allows you to avoid all of those previously mentioned undesirable ingredients. While there is still a chemical process that must be followed to create a hard, usable product, there are many recipes available using more natural, body-friendly ingredients. The basic chemistry of soap making is that there is a reaction between water or liquid, oils and lye. Hearing the word "lye" is sometimes intimidating to those wanting to make a natural product. Many of us believe that lye is harsh, and is just another chemical. In fact, lye is naturally found and created by using the ash from a fire, and draining it through a water process. Lye, in the case of soap making, is simply the reactant to produce the cleaning, and consistency that is needed to make a viable bar of soap. And in fact, once the soap making has gone through the saponification stage (the needed chemical reaction), there is no actual lye left in the soap. The choices of oils that can be used in soap making range from natural lard, to organic coconut or olive oils. Perhaps the most popular of these oils at this time is the Organic Coconut Oil. This oil is not only easily absorbed by the skin, it is extremely moisturizing. In addition, Coconut Oil in the organic form has anti-bacterial properties therefore offering a natural substitute for the undesirable Triclosan. Making your own soap at home gives you the opportunity to incorporate the many benefits of essential oils to not only scent your soap, but also to provide the individual properties associated with each oil. For example, the relaxing effects of Lavender Oil, the invigoration found in Lemon Grass, or the holiday inspiration of smelling a bar of Peppermint scented soap. The use of essential oils lets you be creative and develop your own personal scent for your homemade soap.

The Frugal Satisfaction

While there are many bargains to be found, as well as sales, coupons, and other promotions, on commercially produced soap, there is a definite cost-reduction when making your own soap at home. The initial investment in ingredients may seem like you are spending a lot, but most containers of the needed ingredients will supply you with multiple recipes worth of soap making. Each batch that you make will supply your family with a multitude of bars of natural, wonderfully fragranced, lather filled soap to use for bathing and washing. The utensils you purchase will last for years to come, and the initial cost will recuperate itself very quickly as you discover the benefits of using your own soap. Not only will you save the increasingly difficult to come by dollar, you will also gain an incredible amount of personal satisfaction from making your own soap. The first time you experience the liquids and lye working through saponification, and then the pouring of the soap into molds, you will feel like you have had a major accomplishment. You and your family will revel in the marvellous creation of your homemade soap, as you secretly feel the pride of success and well-being that making your own soap provides.

There is always something to be proud of when you make your own products at home. This is no difference with soap making. As mentioned above, you are able to create a more natural product for you and your family, you will save money doing so, and you will feel a sense of personal satisfaction and well-being from the success of making your own soap.

Chapter 3 - Four Methods Of Making Homemade Soap

Soap-making is an exciting craft that can be put to use as simply a hobby or pastime or as a profitable business or supplemental income. As many people become concerned about what their bodies take in, whether directly or indirectly, the market for natural and handmade products becomes more and more lucrative. This creates a perfect environment for anything homemade, especially body-care products.

Getting started with the craft of homemade soap-making can be just as simple as following a few basic steps. To begin, there are four general methods that are commonly used to make homemade soap.

- Cold process method
- Hot process method
- Rebatch method
- Melt and pour method

Each has its own unique highlights that may make it more suitable or practical for each individual. The rebatch-melt-pour methods for example may work out well for someone who is new to soap making or simply does not have much time to prepare.

Melt and Pour Method

The first and considerably most popular method among newbies, is the melt and pour method. This type of soap making really only involves purchasing a pre made soap base, dicing it up, melting it, adding desired ingredients and additives and placing it into a soap mold. Though it sounds simple enough, this method does have its limitations.

The most common complaint of pre-made bases is that you are at the mercy of the base maker, meaning that you may not always get the "healthiest" base available if that's what you are going for. Likewise, cost is a considerable factor, as it may be significantly cheaper to create your own soap from scratch. If selling a product you have to ensure that you always purchase the same base each and every time, customers need quality and consistency.

The melt and pour method is ideal for people who want to have some hand in the soap making process but don't want to get their hands too dirty. For instance, if you are in the business of selling hair care products, a natural, handmade soap line would definitely compliment your current sale items, but too much time spent on it would take away from your primary focus, hair care. Therefore, in this case, a ready-made soap base would be ideal for expanding your line of products, while not taking away from your current business model.

Cold Process Method

This second method involves working from scratch to produce the pre-made soap base mentioned in the first method. Since a soap base is essentially made up of an oil and an alkali such as lye, when making homemade soap using the cold process you will be saponifying on your own, or combining the oil and the lye in conjunction with the other steps mentioned in the melt and pour method. The biggest difference with the cold process method and the melt and pour is saponification and cure time. With the soap base these things are already taken care of, but when working from scratch, you have to bear the burden of both on your own. The two disadvantages are: the dangers of mixing strong chemicals such as lye in your home and the lengthy cure time. Cure time can last for about 2-6 weeks respectfully.

Hot Process Method

The hot process is very similar to the cold process, and is often a matter of preference with novice soap makers. Some prefer the texture of one type of soap product over the other, but they both share their advantages and disadvantages. The hot process method is often conducted using a crock pot and involves heating the entire mixture throughout the soap making process, from beginning to end. This is considered beneficial in that it speeds up the cure process and allows people to use their soap sooner. But it also requires more monitoring and attention than the cold process. With the cold process the only thing that is heated up is the oil to make it easy to mix, otherwise there is no crockpot like device involved.

The hot process is good for making transparent or liquid soap, as the heat allows the necessary mixture of elements as well as a complete and quick gel phase. The gel phase is the point in which the soap heats up as the chemicals react and is seen as undesirable to some soap makers. To prevent this phase, soap can immediately be refrigerated after it's placed in a mold. Similarly, to promote this phase the soap can be insulated if gelled soap is your preference. It can also be noted that gelled soap can often hold up better to water than ungelled, therefore lasting longer. Generally whether you prefer gelled or hot processed or cold processed will come after your own experimentation and time spent "testing the soap making waters."

Rebatch Method

Lastly, the rebatch method, also called the hand-milled method, is pretty simple and as straightforward as the melt and pour. It involves creating your own unique soap with the scrapings of already made soaps. This again may be desirable for someone who does not have a lot of time to cure or create mixtures from scratch. This method still has a lot of benefits as you can enjoy adding your own essential oils, fragrances, colors and herbs, without the hassle of making a soap base.

Similarly, the rebatch method can also be used with your own soaps made from scratch. It may be beneficial to put to use old soaps or mixtures gone wrong. This can save money and create a quick, and painless soap making procedure if need be.

<u>Helpful recap of the four methods of homemade soap making</u>

Basic Ingredients:

What exactly is needed for each process?

- Soap rebatch method: using already made soap, simply shred it, add desired additives
- Hot process and cold process from scratch: will need lye, fat or heavy oil, scent and color
- Melt and pour method: soap base and desired additives

What are the most important terms I need to know?

- Cure: The process in which the soap sits in the mold in order for excess moisture to exit. Soap needs to be a certain type of "dry" to really be long lasting and beneficial. If this extra moisture doesn't get a chance to exit, you risk your soap falling apart and melting rather quickly.
- Soap base: A mixture of heavy oil such as olive oil, coconut or Shea butter with lye. A soap base is essentially the result of the saponification process.

Saponification: The chemical process that produces soap as a result of the reactions between the fat (heavy oil) and lye.

Chapter 4- The Equipment Needed To Make Homemade Soap

Making your own soap at home is one of the best ways you can work toward living a more frugal life. It is not only financially rewarding, once you are all set up for homemade soap making, you will also find that it is a fun, and very enjoyable, hobby. You can make soap at home to use for yourself and your family, you can make soap to sell at local farmer's markets, craft shows, or on one of the several online craft retailers, or you can make soap to give away as unique, desirable gifts. No matter what you are planning as the end use for your soap, the first step is to gather all of the necessary equipment. There are several items that you will need for soap making, and you will want to use some of them for only soap making. In this chapter I will go through the list of needed equipment, talk about the purpose of each item in soap making, and offer options, where available, for each of the equipment items. You may have some of these items in your kitchen already, but they are all easy to find at either local or online shopping establishments.

The Scale

Possibly the most important tool that you will need for your homemade soap making is the scale. This should be digital, and should read ounces, preferably to the 1/10th ounce. The scale will be used to ensure that the chemical balance of your soap is accurate. You will use it to measure everything including your lye, liquids, oils, and additives. Digital scales can be purchased relatively inexpensively on several websites, or can be found at kitchen or mass merchandise stores.

The Lye Container

When measuring the lye, you will need to have either a clear plastic measuring cup, or bowl that is used only for the lye, and is clearly marked "lye only". Since lye is a toxic substance in the dry form that you will be measuring, it is imperative that this container is used for nothing else. A large measuring cup that will hold at least 12 ounces, depending on the size of the batches you will be making, or a clear plastic bowl, or container, can be found at most any local store. If you are working toward frugality, a check at your local dollar store would be a great place to start looking for this piece of equipment. As with all of the equipment needed for home made soap making, you can also shop from an online soap making retailer for more professional style equipment.

The Mixing Vessel

Mixing your lye and oils together to create your soap requires a stainless steel pot to avoid the chemical reaction that could happen with other metals. One of the best things to use is a stock pot, generally of about an 8 quart size, depending on the size of the batch you are making. Using a stock pot allows you to work down inside the pot to help avoid splashing of the caustic lye substance, prior to saponification. Stainless steel stock pots can be expensive to purchase, but they can be found at a reasonable price at your local mass merchandiser or low price retailer.

Safety

Make sure that you have a pair of safety goggles that cover all around your eyes in case of accidental splashes. The solution is very dangerous prior to saponification and contact with the eyes must be avoided. Safety goggles can be found readily, and inexpensively, at most dollar stores, home improvement stores, or mass merchandisers.

Spoon and Ladle

Mixing, measuring, and pouring, can require either a stainless steel spoon, or a stainless steel ladle. Again, you want these items to be stainless steel to avoid any chemical reaction with the metal. Both of these items are easily found at local dollar or mass merchandise stores.

Stick Blender

This one item, along with the digital scale, is perhaps the most important piece of equipment for making homemade soap. While the mixture of liquids, lye, and oils, can be stirred by hand, the end product will be smoother, harder, and more professional if a stick blender is used. When mixing the ingredients together the stick blender is used to ensure complete integration of all of the parts to result in a timely trace, and ultimately proper saponification, and beautiful bars, of soap. Stick blenders range in price from fairly inexpensive to unnecessarily pricey. For the purpose of soap making, an inexpensive stick blender, which can be found at your local mass merchandise store, is sufficient.

Soap Making

Molds

What you use for a mold for your soap can vary greatly. Everything from dish washing tubs, to plastic storage boxes, to silicone muffin cups, to candy molds can be used. You can also purchase specifically designed soap molds either online or at your local craft store. This is completely up to you, but the recommendation is that you find something that is squared off on the corners rather than rounded to avoid wasting and trimming of your bars. It is also recommended that you find a mold that can either be taken apart to expose the free standing soap, or a mold that is flexible enough to "pop" the soap out upside down. Metal containers should be avoided for this step, with soft plastic, or silicone, being preferable.

Miscellaneous Tools

The only other things you may need for your homemade soap making project will include paper towels, stainless steel measuring spoons for measuring scents and essential oils, a few small measuring cups, or bowls, to hold ingredients prior to adding them to the soap mixture, or a small whisk for adding essential oils. These items may already be in your kitchen, or can be found at any dollar or mass merchandise store.

While it may seem like a long list of items that you need to make soap, remember that these are one time purchases that will allow you to make a life time of unique and creative soaps. As with any craft or hobby, the tools you use will determine the quality of the end product. Don't hesitate to set yourself up for success by having the proper soap making equipment.

Chapter 5 - Safety Measures To Take When Making Homemade Soap

Creating soap is a craft mankind has been perfecting for centuries. Although the modern day human is more apt to go down to a local shop to buy soap, there are many individuals who prefer making it by hand at home as a hobby or for profit. Soap making is easy; however it is important to acknowledge potentially harmful products and processes used to create it.

Mindy Jackson
How to Handle Lye Properly

A form of potash known as lye, or caustic soda, is a major ingredient in soap making. Unfortunately lye is highly toxic if consumed, will corrode if exposed to skin, and will blind if splashed into the eyes. Fortunately, lye is easy to manage and handle as long as the user is instructed on how to use it properly. When creating the lye-water make sure to add the lye to the water a little at a time, not the reverse. If water is added to lye then the liquid will sputter or even explode out of the container potentially harming the soap-maker.

It is important to note that a soap-maker should only buy pure lye. Using drain cleaner or other products that list lye as an ingredient will create an extremely inferior product and damage the skin.

Always store the lye in an air tight container that is clearly labeled and kept out of reach of children or pets. Be sure that the Material Safety Data Sheet (MSDS) that comes with the lye is always present in case of emergencies.

Choosing the Right Equipment

The next important thing to do is to select the right materials to use in creating the soap. Choose a large enough container that will keep the liquid in even when being stirred. It is also recommended to use a tall graduated pitcher or cylinder when mixing lye-water because it will help contain the fumes. All containers exposed to heat must be able to withstand heat up to 200-degrees Fahrenheit. Any container that cracks, breaks, or melts at this temperature must not be used. Never use any containers or spoons made of tin, zinc, or aluminum because lye will react chemically to these metals.

Organize the Tools

It is important to keep all of the soap making equipment clearly labeled to reduce the chances of confusion when crafting the soap. While preparing to make soap, check the equipment that is about to be used to be sure that there are no cracks or residue left from previous sessions. These containers, pitchers, and spoons should only be used for soap making and not for food related purposes.

The Ideal Work Space

Soap making can be a very messy process, so be sure the workspace is clean at all times. Lye is not only corrosive to human tissues but also various other surfaces like wood or linoleum. Line counters with old newspapers to keep them safe from potential damage and for an easy clean up in case anything spills. Because vinegar is an acid it will quickly neutralize lye, one must always keep a large bottle of white vinegar in the workspace at all times to use for any accidents. If lye spills on a person, the floor, or any other surface, simply pour vinegar on it to neutralize the lye, and then clean with cold water.

Secure all pets and keep all small children away from the workplace while crafting the soap. If someone is distracted while working he/she is more apt to make mistakes.

Fully Cover the Body

When handling lye, one must always use safety goggles and thick plastic gloves that cover as much of the arms as possible. It is not wise to wear long sleeves because fabric will absorb the lye and trap it against the skin.

Heavy shoes and thick pants are also recommended to reduce the chances of lye being absorbed through the feet or legs. Additionally, some soap-makers choose to wear a face mask to prevent breathing in harmful fumes created when adding lye to water.

Clean Up

Once the mixing process is finished, clean all soap making equipment thoroughly. Always begin cleansing the equipment immediately following the mixing process while the soap is still soft for an easier clean up. Fill the sink with hot water and add a squirt of dish washing detergent along with half a cup of vinegar. Scrape down the pots and pitchers well so that no soap residue remains. If a rag is necessary for a thorough cleaning, leave it out for at least twenty four hours before throwing it in the washing machine.

Drying the Soap

The process of soap-making, also known as saponification, neutralizes the lye in the soap. In order for this process to occur, the soap must rest for a period of time to 'cure' so that no lye remains in the soap. It is recommended that the soap lay out on a drying rack for a minimum of three weeks to insure that no lye remains.

There are many reasons why someone would make their soap by hand. Some want to abstain from the harsh chemicals used in commercial soaps. Others are sensitive to the strong fragrances and wish to develop alternatives to the stronger scented commercial soaps. Regardless of the reasons an individual begins his/her foray into the art and science of soap-making, it is of the utmost importance to understand the process completely and understand the hazards associated with the various ingredients.

Chapter 6 - Adding Colors And Scents To Homemade Soap

Pure is Always Better

Once the hobby of making your own pure and chemical-free soap enters your mind and psyche, the average woman (or man) will not waste any time in beginning. In case you have not yet begun, and achieving melted glycerin is still a mystery, this chapter will comfortably introduce you to liquefying glycerin for soap. Use 1/4 lb glycerin blocks for soap base, and melt in your microwave safe glass container for 25 seconds. You can also melt in a glass pot on stove top. The key factor is that the glycerin should only melt and not ever bubble. Select plastic molds such as for candy or candles to harden the soaps in when complete. Have a wooden spoon or spatula and a ceramic stirrer used only for your soap or candle mixing.

Soap Making

<u>*The Basic Start Up*</u>

Starting with 1/4 lb. glycerin blocks which you melt on stove top or in the microwave in glass pots, begin your soap. Do not let the glycerin reach the bubbling stage as it will decrease the bubbling of your finished soap. It is wise to remove from the heat source when a few pieces of the glycerin blocks are still intact, and then mixing them thoroughly with a wooden spoon or soap mixer until smooth and completely melted. Line up your plastic soap molds. It is at this stage you are ready to add color or fragrance to your product.

<u>*Adding Fragrances to Handmade Soap*</u>

Initially, it is very beneficial to utilize fragrances that bring their own color with them. Vanilla is a popular fragrance and results in the glycerin taking on a light yellow to dark brown hue, dependent upon the amount used. It will take a little experimentation to determine the exact strength of fragrance you want for your soap. The average ratio is 1/2 teaspoon fragrance into 1/4 lb glycerin. Boiled coffee or tea provide their scents in soap, as will olive oil, certain flowers and cinnamon, rosemary and other herbs. Eucalyptus is a strong scent often associated with aiding asthma or sinus cold sufferers. Each variety of citrus provides its individual scent and some of its color as well.

When purchasing oils for your scents, the selections are fragrance oils and essential oils. Select essential oils, even though higher priced, because they are much longer lasting and have better strength. There is a limitless amount of lovely and intoxicating scents available at your drug store, grocery or online. These purchased scents can be mixed in varying ratios with your own ingenuity and new fragrances are born.

You may want to choose fragrances similar to cooking or baking aromas, achieve one that is similar to your personal fragrance in toiletries, or the natural scents of flowers, foods and grasses. They are all at your disposal with either essential oils or the less expensive fragrance oils. If some combinations of fragrance and color leave an ash residue on your soap, this can be easily brushed or cut off after hardening. Now it is time to add extra color if desired.

Adding Colors to Handmade Soap

Many herbs are a natural color for your soaps. Herbs such as chamomile, rosehips and peppermint all delightfully release their color in oil. Their oils also retain the color through cold process soap making. Some herbs add color and texture to soap when the dried herb is stirred into the soap. Good herbs to use in soap are powdered sandalwood which gives light brown, powdered patchouli for a richer brown, calendula petals impart a yellow, and ground rose hips provide pinks and red to your soap.

Some of the natural herbs will not keep their color, so always pre-test your herbs in a small batch of soap before making a large batch. You can buy herbs from herb companies or purchase them online soap making suppliers, health stores and groceries. Some natural and health vendors sell various fruit fibers for use as natural soap colorants. Berry fibers add shades of pink to soap. Dried clays can be added to soap for good color. Two excellent ones for soap color are French green clay for a pale green and French pink clay for pink.

FD&C colors and iron oxides add vivid and bright colors to your soap. FD&C colors should be used with melt and pour soaps for best results. Micas will always add shimmer and sparkle to soap. Many hobby manufacturers sell kits for these unique, novel and special treatments for your handmade soap products. Hobby and craft stores regularly carry an assortment of accessories and aids for soap making.

Therein tells the tale of handmade soap without the inexplicable harshness of commercial soaps and without the high price. You can finally know without a doubt exactly what you are washing your face with, and what the ingredients are in your children's bath soap. No longer will you wonder about skin dryness, chapping or redness, because they won't happen with your handmade glycerin and herbal or floral soap. You can say farewell to sudden breakouts. Especially important, anyone who progresses well in soap making by hand finds the handmade items reflect great care and kindness when presented as thoughtful gifts. They are personable and loving gifts for cheerful get well baskets or for Birthday and Mother's Day arrangements.

Chapter 7 - Great Homemade Soap Recipes

Soap is a product that we all hopefully use. It is one of the few items that is fairly universal, yet so different. Soap can clean or damage skin depending on the type. Some nourishes skin, some dries out skin, and some perfumes skin, but it is all meant to clean you in some way, and most have harsh chemicals that don't need to be in them.

Making your own soap at home is not just a way to save you some money, but it is a way to individualize your soap to what you actually want to be on your body, and more importantly, a way to get rid of the unnecessary filler chemicals that are in your typical over-the-counter bar of soap. Homemade soap also makes great gifts for everyone from family members to teachers. Below are some of the best do-it-yourself soap ideas.

Citrus and Herb Body Soap

Citrus is a natural cleanser, that's why it is found in everything from laundry detergent, to chemical cleaners, to dishwasher soap. Naturally that same citrus cleanser can be used to make your own, incredible effective, homemade body soap.

Ingredients:

- Glycerin Soap
- 3 Lemons

- 3 Oranges (or any other citrus you prefer)
- 3 tbs. Basil
- 3 tbs. Rosemary (or any other herb you prefer)
- Utensils
- Plastic Spoon
- Glass Mixing Bowl
- Grater
- Soap Mold

Step 1

Dice your herbs, they can be substituted for any herbs you prefer, and make sure you get rid of any excess moisture by squeezing the cut herbs in a paper towel or napkin.

Step 2

Zest the peal of your citrus and make a good pile out of it, a cheese grater works great if you don't have a zester. For every cup of citrus peel used, you will use 1 tbsp. of your herbs.

Step 3

Melt the soap blocks in the glass mixing bowl. Only melt for 20 seconds at a time and stir each time until the soap is fully melted.

Step 4

Add the citrus and herb to the melted soap. It is important you keep gently stirring to make sure nothing settles at the bottom. The color can be tricky here so add the amount of different citruses and herbs you like until the color is nice. The average is one cup of citrus to 1 tbsp. of herbs, but this is about you and what you like. Play with the combination until you have something that works for you.

Step 5

Mold the citrus. Pour the mixture into the mold of your choice. Common molds are simple plastic containers, but you can even get creative for holidays and buy specially designed plastic molds. Let the mold sit overnight to fully harden. Alternately, if you are in a hurry you can freeze the mold for about an hour, and enjoy!

Oatmeal Body Soap

Oatmeal soap is an age old secret to homemade soap. The oatmeal works as a scrub so you aren't just getting clean but you are exfoliating as well. This is a great soap for scenting and coloring the way you want, and so simple that you don't end up with more additives than necessary.

Ingredients:

- 8-16 cubes Goat's Milk Soap Suspension Formula
- Almond Oil Extract (or the extract of your choice)
- 1/2 Cup Oatmeal

- Utensils
- Glass Bowl
- Spoon
- Soap Mold

Step 1

Dice the Oatmeal so it is a little grainier. Some stores do sell oatmeal this way, but if you simply have traditional oatmeal, mix it a little in a processor or dice it somehow to make it a bit smaller.

Step 2

Place the Goats Milk Soap in a microwave safe bowl and microwave for anywhere from one to three minutes until it is melted. IMPORTANT: make sure you stir the soap every 30 seconds to keep it from burning, boiling, and unevenly melting.

Step 3

Add the extract to the melted soap and mix. You will want to add about 6 drops for every cube of soap you melted. Of course this is personal to you so if you want more or less extract, use more or less, but make sure not to go overboard.

Step 4

Add the oatmeal. You will want to add 1/4 cup for every 8 cubes of soap you melted. Again, this is a guideline, not a hard fast rule, increase or decrease the amount based on what you want. Be careful though not to add so much that the soap doesn't harden right and breaks apart.

Step 5

Pour the soap into the mixture of your choice and let sit until hardened. This can be as fast as an hour or as long as four. Once this is done your soap is complete.

Soap Making
Decorate

Now that you have gotten two great soap ideas, it is time to decorate them. A pretty ribbon, some twine, colorful napkins, or even cling wrap all work well for displaying this soap. It is homemade and displays nicely on its own, so don't go over the top, but this is the perfect gift for someone else or simply for you to use in your own home to save money.

About The Author

Mindy Jackson is an individual who takes pride in doing various projects. It could be crafting or even woodworking, whatever it is, she is willing to learn all about it. It is no surprise that when she learned about homemade soap making that she was immediately interested in learning all about it and eager to make her first batch of soap.

Mindy has used her book as a medium to share her experience with her readers and also to highlight all the benefits that they can get from making their own soap.

www.ingramcontent.com/pod-product-compliance
Ingram Content Group UK Ltd.
Pitfield, Milton Keynes, MK11 3LW, UK
UKHW022219230426
12048UKWH00016BA/937